The 90s Ten Years Of Hits

KEYBOARD CHORD SONG BOOK

GW00370560

Wise Publications
London/New York/Sydney/Paris/Copenhagen/Madrid/Tokyo

Exclusive distributors:
Music Sales Limited
8/9 Frith Street,
London W1D 3JB, England.
Music Sales Pty Limited
120 Rothschild Avenue
Rosebery, NSW 2018,
Australia.

Order No. AM962841
ISBN 0-7119-8045-4
This book © Copyright 2000 by Wise Publications

Book design by Chloë Alexander
Music arranged & engraved by Roger Day
Compiled by Nick Crispin

Photographs courtesy of EastWest Records.

Printed in the United Kingdom by
Printwise (Haverhill) Limited, Haverhill, Suffolk.

Your Guarantee of Quality
As publishers, we strive to produce every book to the highest
commercial standards. The music has been freshly engraved and
the book has been carefully designed to minimise awkward page
turns and to make playing from it a real pleasure. Particular care
has been given to specifying acid-free, neutral-sized paper made
from pulps which have not been elemental chlorine bleached. This
pulp is from farmed sustainable forests and was produced with
special regard for the environment. Throughout, the printing and
binding have been planned to ensure a sturdy, attractive
publication which should give years of enjoyment. If your copy
fails to meet our high standards, please inform us and we will
gladly replace it.

Music Sales' complete catalogue describes thousands of titles and
is available in full colour sections by subject, direct from Music
Sales Limited. Please state your areas of interest and send a
cheque/postal order for £1.50 for postage to: Music Sales Limited,
Newmarket Road, Bury St. Edmunds, Suffolk IP33 3YB.

www.musicsales.com

Angels

Words & Music by Robbie Williams & Guy Chambers

Verse 1

E
  I sit and wait.

                                   Asus2 A   C#m/A
Does another angel contemplate my fate?

B   E
  And do they know the places where we go

                         Asus2 A   C#m/A
When we're grey and old?_____

B   F#m7
  Cos I have been told

           A   C#m7
That salva-tion lets their wings unfold.

A   D
  So when I'm lying in my bed,

             A/C#   A
Thoughts running through my head

        E
And I feel that love is dead,

D   A/C#   E
  I'm loving angels instead.

Chorus 1

                    B   C#m
And through it all she offers me protection,

                    A
A lot of love and affection,

Asus2   E
Whether I'm right or wrong.

                    B
And down the waterfall,

                C#m
Wherever it may take me,

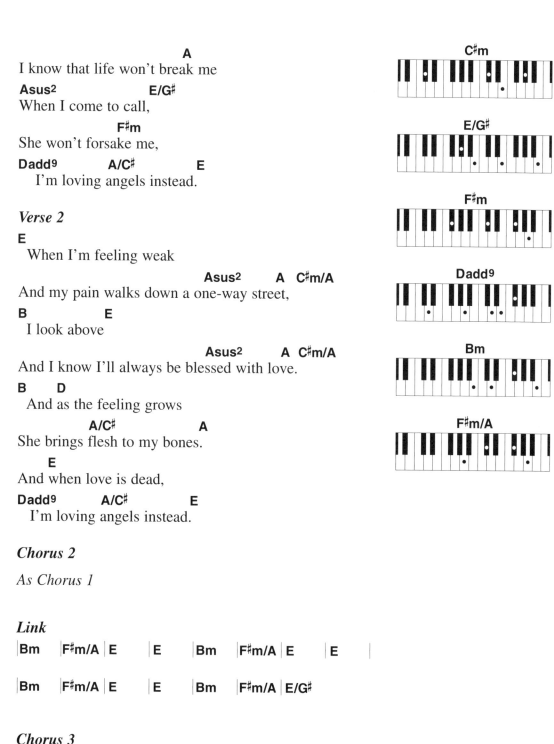

              A
I know that life won't break me
Asus2   **E/G♯**
When I come to call,
         F♯m
She won't forsake me,
Dadd9   **A/C♯**   **E**
  I'm loving angels instead.

Verse 2

E
  When I'm feeling weak
                Asus2   **A** **C♯m/A**
And my pain walks down a one-way street,
B   **E**
 I look above
               Asus2   **A** **C♯m/A**
And I know I'll always be blessed with love.
B   **D**
  And as the feeling grows
      A/C♯   **A**
She brings flesh to my bones.
   E
And when love is dead,
Dadd9   **A/C♯**   **E**
  I'm loving angels instead.

Chorus 2

As Chorus 1

Link

|**Bm** |**F♯m/A** **E** |**E** |**Bm** |**F♯m/A** **E** |**E** |

|**Bm** |**F♯m/A** **E** |**E** |**Bm** |**F♯m/A** |**E/G♯**

Chorus 3

As Chorus 1

Baby One More Time

Words & Music by Max Martin

Cm

G7

B♭/D

E♭

Fm

Gsus4

G

A♭

B♭

Intro

N.C.
　　　　Oh baby, baby! Oh baby, baby!

Verse 1

Cm　　　　　　　　　　**G7**　　　　　　**B♭/D E♭**
Oh baby, baby, how was I supposed to know

　　　　Fm　　　　　　**G7   Cm**
That something wasn't right here?

　　　　　　　　　　　G7　　　　**B♭/D E♭**
Oh baby, baby, I shouldn't have let you go.

　　　Fm　　　　　　**G7   Cm**
And now you're out of sight, yeah.

　　　　　　　　　　　　　G7
Show me how you want it to be,

　　　E♭　　　　　　　　**Fm**　　　**G7   Cm**
Tell me baby, cos I need to know now, oh because

Chorus 1

Cm　　　　　　　**G7**
　My loneliness is killin' me

　　　E♭　　　　　　**Fm**　　　**Gsus4 G**
And I, I must confess I still believe,   still believe.

Cm　　　　　　　　　　　**G7**
　When I'm not with you I lose my mind.

A♭　　**B♭**　**E♭**
Give me a sign,_____

Fm　　　　**G7**　　　**Cm**
Hit me baby one more time.

Verse 2

Cm　　　　　　　　　　**G7**　　　　**B♭/D E♭**
　Oh baby, baby, the reason I breathe is you.

Fm　　　　**G7   Cm**
Boy, you got me blinded.

            G7   **B♭/D E♭**

Oh pretty baby, there's nothing that I wouldn't do,

  Fm   **G7**   **Cm**

It's not the way I planned it.

                   G7

Show me how you want it to be,

  E♭   **Fm**   **G7** **Cm**

Tell me baby, cos I need to know now, oh because

Chorus 2

Cm   **G7**

  My loneliness is killin' me

    E♭   **Fm**   **Gsus4 G**

And I, I must confess I still believe,   still believe.

Cm   **G7**

  When I'm not with you I lose my mind.

A♭   **B♭**   **E♭**

Give me a sign,____

Cm   **G**   **Cm**

Hit me baby one more time.

Link

N.C.

  Oh baby, baby. Oh, oh.

Oh baby, baby. Ah, yeah, yeah.

Bridge

Cm   **G7**   **E♭/B♭**

  Oh baby, baby, how was I supposed to know?

Fm   **Gsus4 G**

A♭   **B♭**   **Fm7**

  Oh pretty baby, I shouldn't have let you go.___

A♭ B♭   **Cm**   **G7**   **E♭**

  I must confess that my loneliness is killin' me now.__

       Fm   **Gsus4 G**   **A♭**

Don't you know I still   believe

              B♭   **A♭maj7** **E♭/G**

That you will be here and give me a sign?

Fm   **B♭**   **G7/B**

Hit me baby one more time.

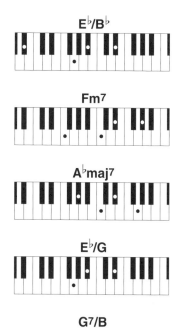

Chorus 3

Cm   **G7**
  My loneliness is killin' me

      E♭   **Fm**   **Gsus4 G**
And I, I must confess I still believe,   still believe.

Cm   **G7**
  When I'm not with you I lose my mind.

A♭   **B♭**   **E♭**
Give me a sign,_____

Fm   **G7**   **Cm**
Hit me baby one more time.

Chorus 4

Cm   **G7**
  My loneliness is killin' me

      E♭   **Fm**   **Gsus4 G**
And I, I must confess I still believe,   still believe.

Cm   **G7**
  When I'm not with you I lose my mind.

A♭   **B♭**   **E♭**
Give me a sign,_____

Cm   **G**   **Cm**
Hit me baby one more time.

Don't Look Back In Anger

Words & Music by Noel Gallagher

C

F

G

Am

E

Fm6

A♭dim

Intro

| C | | F | | C | F | ‖

Verse 1

C   G   Am
Slip inside the eye of your mind,
              E   F
Don't you know you might find
G   C   Am   G
  A better place to play.
C   G   Am
You said that you'd never been,
            E   F
But all the things that you've seen
G   C   Am   G
  Slowly fade away.

Bridge 1

F   Fm6   C
  So I start a revolution from my bed
         F   Fm6   C
Cos you said the brains I had went to my head.
F   Fm6   C
Step outside, summertime's in bloom,
G
Stand up beside the fireplace,
A♭dim
Take that look from off your face,
Am   G   F   G
You ain't never gonna burn my heart out.___

Chorus 1

```
C  G          Am
So Sally can wait,
      E            F          G      C   Am G
She knows it's too late as we're walking on by.
     C   G      Am
Her soul slides away,
E              F        G          C      G
  But don't look back in anger, I heard you say.
|Am   E   |F   G   |C   Am G ‖
```

Verse 2

```
C            G              Am
Take me to the place where you go,
      E         F
Where nobody knows
G              C     Am G
  If it's night or day.
C                  G        Am
Please don't put your life in the hands
      E          F
Of a rock 'n' roll band
G                  C     Am G
  Who'll throw it all away.
```

Bridge 2

```
F                  Fm6          C
  I'm gonna start a revolution from my head
        F           Fm6         C
Cos you said the brains I had went to my head.
F          Fm6         C
Step outside, the summertime's in bloom,
G
Stand up beside the fireplace,
A♭dim
Take that look from off your face,
     Am            G       F       G
Cos you ain't never gonna burn my heart out.___
```

Chorus 2

C G   Am
So Sally can wait,

    E   F   G   C   Am G
She knows it's too late as she's walking on by.

    C   G   Am
My soul slides away,

E   F   G   C   Am G
  But don't look back in anger, I heard you say.

Bridge 3

|F   Fm6 |C |F   Fm6 |C |F   Fm6 |C |

|G |A♭dim |Am G |F |G |G ||

Chorus 3

C G   Am
So Sally can wait,

    E   F   G   C   Am G
She knows it's too late as we're walking on by.

    C   G   Am
Her soul slides away,

E   F   G   C   Am G
  But don't look back in anger, I heard you say.

Chorus 4

C G   Am
So Sally can wait,

    E   F   G   C   Am G
She knows it's too late as she's walking on by.

    C   G   Am
My soul slides away,

                  F
But don't look back in anger,

       Fm6   C G
Don't look back in anger, I heard you say.

|Am E |F   Fm6   C
                  It's not too late.

Frozen

Words & Music by Madonna & Patrick Leonard

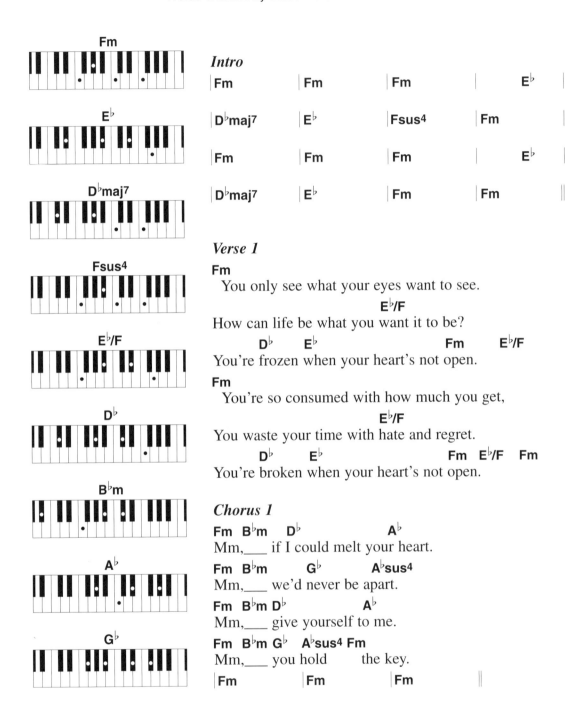

Fm

E♭

D♭maj7

Fsus4

E♭/F

D♭

B♭m

A♭

G♭

Intro

| Fm | Fm | Fm | | E♭ |

| D♭maj7 | E♭ | Fsus4 | Fm |

| Fm | Fm | Fm | | E♭ |

| D♭maj7 | E♭ | Fm | Fm ‖

Verse 1

Fm
  You only see what your eyes want to see.
                           E♭/F
How can life be what you want it to be?
             D♭   **E♭**   **Fm**   **E♭/F**
You're frozen when your heart's not open.
Fm
  You're so consumed with how much you get,
                            E♭/F
You waste your time with hate and regret.
             D♭   **E♭**   **Fm** **E♭/F** **Fm**
You're broken when your heart's not open.

Chorus 1

Fm B♭m   D♭   A♭
Mm,___ if I could melt your heart.
Fm B♭m   G♭   A♭sus4
Mm,___ we'd never be apart.
Fm B♭m D♭   A♭
Mm,___ give yourself to me.
Fm B♭m G♭ A♭sus4 Fm
Mm,___ you hold   the key.

| Fm | Fm | Fm | ‖

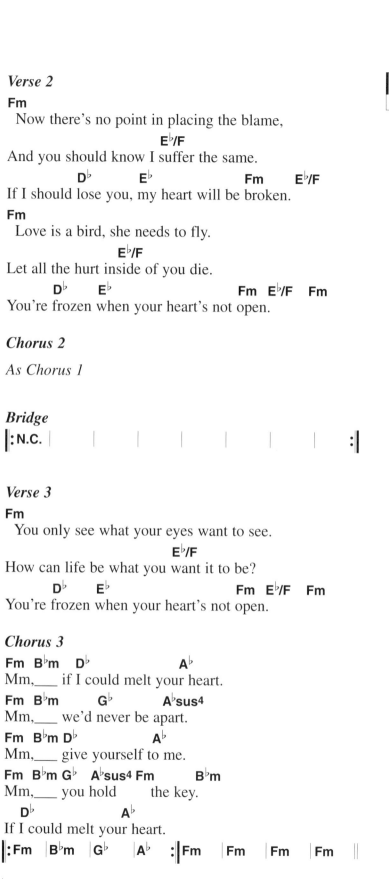
Verse 2

Fm
  Now there's no point in placing the blame,
                  E♭/F
And you should know I suffer the same.
       D♭   **E♭**   **Fm**   **E♭/F**
If I should lose you, my heart will be broken.
Fm
  Love is a bird, she needs to fly.
             E♭/F
Let all the hurt inside of you die.
      D♭   **E♭**   **Fm E♭/F** **Fm**
You're frozen when your heart's not open.

Chorus 2

As Chorus 1

Bridge

‖: **N.C.** | | | | | | | :‖

Verse 3

Fm
  You only see what your eyes want to see.
               E♭/F
How can life be what you want it to be?
      D♭   **E♭**   **Fm E♭/F** **Fm**
You're frozen when your heart's not open.

Chorus 3

Fm B♭m D♭   **A♭**
Mm,___ if I could melt your heart.
Fm B♭m   **G♭**   **A♭sus4**
Mm,___ we'd never be apart.
Fm B♭m D♭   **A♭**
Mm,___ give yourself to me.
Fm B♭m G♭ **A♭sus4 Fm**   **B♭m**
Mm,___ you hold   the key.
    D♭   **A♭**
If I could melt your heart.
‖: **Fm** |**B♭m** |**G♭** |**A♭** :‖**Fm** |**Fm** |**Fm** |**Fm** ‖

The Day We Caught The Train

Words & Music by Steve Cradock, Damon Minchella, Oscar Harrison & Simon Fowler

Em

D

G

F

E

C

B

A

A♯dim

Verse 1

Em   **D**
Never saw it as the start,

               G
It's more a change of heart.

F
Rapping on the windows,

                             E
Whistling down the chimney pot.

G   **D**
Blowing off the dust in the room where I forgot,

  C   **B**
I laid my plans in solid rock.

Em
Stepping through the door like a troubadour,

                 A
Whiling just an hour away.

Em
Looking at the trees on the roadside,

           A
Feeling it's a holiday.

Chorus 1

D   **A♯dim**
You and I should ride the coast

         Bm   **A/C♯**   **Em**
And wind up in our favourite coats just miles away.

G
  Roll a number,

                        A
Write another song like Jimmy heard

                        D
The day he caught the train.

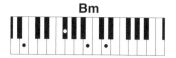

Bm

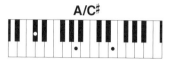

A/C#

Link 1

    A   G   Em   D
Oh _ la la,   oh _ la la,

    A   G   Em
Oh _ la la,   oh _ la.

Verse 2

Em   **D**
  He sipped another rum and Coke

        G
And told a dirty joke.

F
Walking like Groucho,

              E
Sucking on a number 10.

G   **D**
Rolling on the floor with the cigarette burns walked in,

     C   **B**
I'll miss the crush and I'm home again.

Em
Stepping through the door with the night in store,

            A
Whiling just an hour away.

Em
Step into the sky in the star bright

         A
Feeling it's a brighter day.

Chorus 2

As Chorus 1

Link 2

As Link 1

15

Middle

A

  You and I should ride the tracks

                                                   D

And find ourselves just wading through tomorrow.

A

  And you and I when we're coming down,

                                                   D

We're only getting back and you know I feel no sorrow.

Link 3

‖: **D**   **A**   **G**   **Em**   **D**
   Oh _ la la,   oh _ la la,

     A   **G**   **Em**   :‖
Oh _ la la,   oh _ la.

Bridge

‖: **D**   **A**
   When you find that things are getting wild,

      G   **Em**   :‖ *Play 4 times*
But don't you want days like these?

Outro

‖: **D**   **A**   **G**   **Em**   **D**
   Oh _ la la,   oh _ la la,

     A   **G**   **Em**   :‖ *Repeat to fade*
Oh _ la la,   oh _ la.

Killing Me Softly

Words by Norman Gimbel. Music by Charles Fox

Em

Chorus 1

N.C.

Strumming my pain with his fingers,

Singing my life with his words,

Am

Killing me softly with his song,

Killing me softly with his song,

D

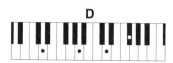

Telling my whole life with his words,

Killing me softly with his song.

G

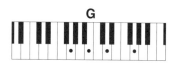

Instrumental

| **N.C.** | | | | |

| **N.C.** | | | | ‖

A

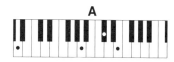

Verse 1

N.C.

I heard he sang a good song,

C

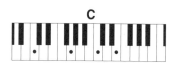

I heard he had a smile,

And so I came to see him

And listen for a while.

F

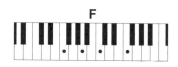

And there he was, this young boy,

E

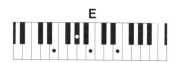

A stranger to my eyes.

Chorus 2

Em   **Am**
Strumming my pain with his fingers, (one time)
D   **G**
Singing my life with his words, (two times)
Em   **A**
Killing me softly with his song,
                          D   **C**
Killing me softly with his song,
                                G   **C**
Telling my whole life with his words,
                      F   **E**
Killing me softly with his song.

Verse 2
N.C.
I felt all flushed with fever,

Embarrassed by the crowd,

I felt he found my letters

And read each one out loud.

I prayed that he would finish

But he just kept right on…

Chorus 3

Em   **Am**
Strumming my pain with his fingers, (one time)
D   **G**
Singing my life with his words, (two times)
Em   **A**
Killing me softly with his song,
                          D   **C**
Killing me softly with his song,
                                G   **C**
Telling my whole life with his words,
                      F   **E**
Killing me softly with his song.

Bridge

Em   A   D   G
Oh_____ oh_____

Em   A
La la la la la la

   D   C
Woh___ la____

   G   C   F   E
Woh___ la_____ la____

Chorus 3

‖: **Em   Am**
   Strumming my pain with his fingers,

D   G
Singing my life with his words,

Em   A
Killing me softly with his song,

     D   C
Killing me softly with his song,

     G   C
Telling my whole life with his words,

   F   E   :‖ *Repeat to fade*
Killing me softly with his song._____

I Will Always Love You

Words & Music by Dolly Parton

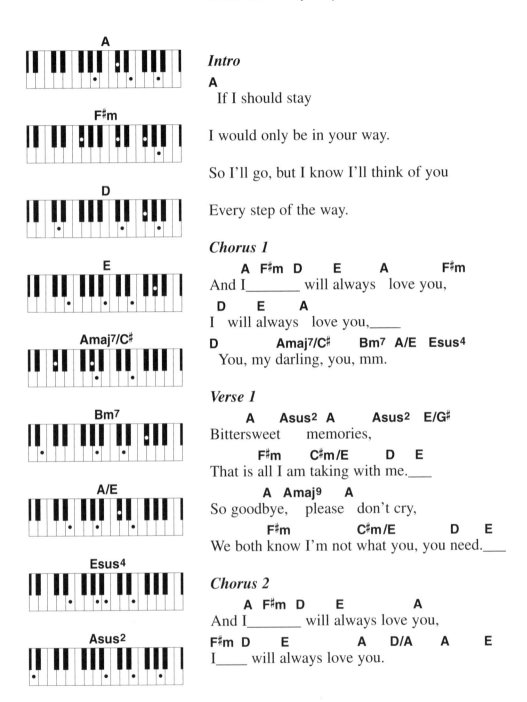

Intro

A

　　If I should stay

I would only be in your way.

So I'll go, but I know I'll think of you

Every step of the way.

Chorus 1

　　　　A　F#m　D　　E　　　A　　　　F#m
And I_____ will always　 love you,
　　　D　　　E　　　A
I　will always　 love you,_____
　　D　　　　　　Amaj7/C#　　　Bm7　A/E　Esus4
　You, my darling, you, mm.

Verse 1

　　　　A　　Asus2　A　　　Asus2　E/G#
Bittersweet　　　 memories,
　　　　　F#m　　C#m/E　　　D　　E
That is all I am taking with me.____
　　　　　A　Amaj9　　A
So goodbye,　　please　 don't cry,
　　　　　　F#m　　　　　C#m/E　　　　D　　E
We both know I'm not what you, you need.___

Chorus 2

　　　　A　F#m　D　　E　　　　　　A
And I_____ will always love you,
　F#m　D　　E　　　　　　　A　　D/A　　A　　　E
I____ will always love you.

Instrumental

| A | D/A | A | E/G♯ |

| F♯m | C♯m/E | D | E | |

| A | Amaj9 | A | C♯m7 |

| F♯m | C♯m/E | D | E | ‖

Verse 2

  A D/A   A
I hope life treats you kind
E/G♯ F♯m   C♯m/E   D   E
And I hope you have all you dreamed of._____
        A   Amaj9   A   C♯m7
And I wish you joy and happiness.
        F♯m   C♯m/E D   E
But above all this, I wish you love.____

Chorus 3

   B G♯m E F♯   B
And I_____ will always love you,
G♯m E F♯   B
I will al - ways love you,
 G♯m E F♯   B
I will al - ways love you,
 G♯m E F♯   B G♯m
I will al - ways love you,_____
E   F♯   B   G♯m
I will always love you,_____
E   F♯ G♯m F♯/A♯   E
I, I will al - ways   love you,___ you.
       Bmaj7/D♯
Darling, I love you.
      F♯sus4   F♯   B
Ooh, I'll always, I'll always love you.

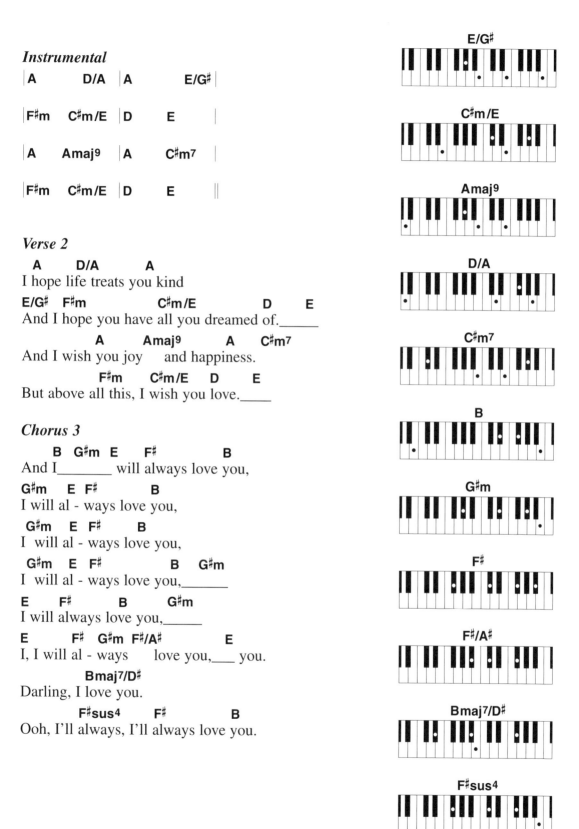

E/G♯

C♯m/E

Amaj9

D/A

C♯m7

B

G♯m

F♯

F♯/A♯

Bmaj7/D♯

F♯sus4

Never Ever

Words & Music by Shaznay Lewis, Esmail Jazayeri & Sean Mather

D♭

D♭7

G♭

A♭

A♭7

D♭/F

E♭m7

G

Intro (*spoken*)

D♭
  A few questions that I need to know,

D♭7
  How could you ever hurt me so?

G♭
  I need to know what I've done wrong

D♭
  And how long it's been going on.

Was it that I never paid enough attention

D♭7
  Or did I not give enough affection?

A♭
  Not only will your answers keep me sane

A♭7
  But I'll know never to make the same mistake again.

D♭
  You can tell me to my face,

D♭7
  Or even on the phone,

G♭
  You can write it in a letter,

D♭
  Either way I have to know.

Did I never treat you right?

A♭
  Did I always start the fight?

G♭   **D♭/F**   **E♭m7**
Either way I'm going out of my mind.

D♭
  All the answers to my questions I have to find.

Verse 1 *(sung)*

D♭
  My head's spinning,
D♭7
  Boy I'm in a daze,
G♭
  I feel so isolated,
D♭
  Don't want to communicate.

I'll take a shower, I will scour,
D♭7
  I will run,
A♭
  Find peace of mind,
A♭7
The happy mind I once owned, yeah.
D♭
Flexin' vocabulary runs right through me,
D♭7
  The alphabet runs right from A to Z.
G♭
  Conversations, hesitations in my mind,
D♭
  You got my conscience asking questions that I can't find.

I'm not crazy,
     A♭   G
I'm sure I ain't done nothing wrong, no.
G♭   D♭/F E♭m7
  I'm just waiting
      D♭
Cos I heard that this feeling won't last that long.

Chorus 1

D♭
  Never ever have I felt so low,
D♭7
  When you gonna take me out of this black hole?
G♭
  Never ever have I felt so sad,
D♭
  The way I'm feeling, yeah, you got me feeling really bad.

  Never ever have I had to find,
D♭7
  I've had to dig away to find my own peace of mind.
A♭
  I never ever had my conscience to fight,
A♭7
  The way I'm feeling, yeah, it just don't feel right.
D♭
  Never ever have I ever felt so low,
D♭7
  When you gonna take me out of this black hole?
G♭
  Never ever have I ever felt so sad,
D♭
  The way I'm feelin', yeah, you got me feeling really bad.

Never ever have I had to find,
A♭   **G**
  I've had to dig away to find my own peace of mind.
G♭   **D♭/F**   **E♭m7**
  I never ever had my conscience to fight,
D♭   **A♭**
  The way I'm feeling, yeah, it just don't feel right.

Verse 2

D♭
  I keep searching
D♭7
  Deep within my soul
G♭
  For all the answers,

24

D♭
  Don't wanna hurt no more.

I need peace, got to feel at ease,
D♭7
  Need to be
A♭
  Free from pain, go insane,
A♭7
  My heart aches.
D♭
Sometimes vocabulary runs through my head,
D♭7
  The alphabet runs right from A to Z.
G♭
  Conversations, hesitations in my mind,
D♭
  You got my conscience asking questions that I can't find.

I'm not crazy,
      A♭   **G**
I'm sure I ain't done nothing wrong,
G♭   **D♭/F E♭m7**
Now I'm just waiting
       D♭
Cos I heard that this feeling won't last that long.

Chorus 2

As Chorus 1

Outro

‖:   **N.C.**
  You can tell me to my face,

You can tell me on the phone,

Ooh, you can write it in a letter babe,
                            :‖   *Repeat to fade*
Cos I really need to know.

No Matter What

Words by Jim Steinman. Music by Andrew Lloyd Webber

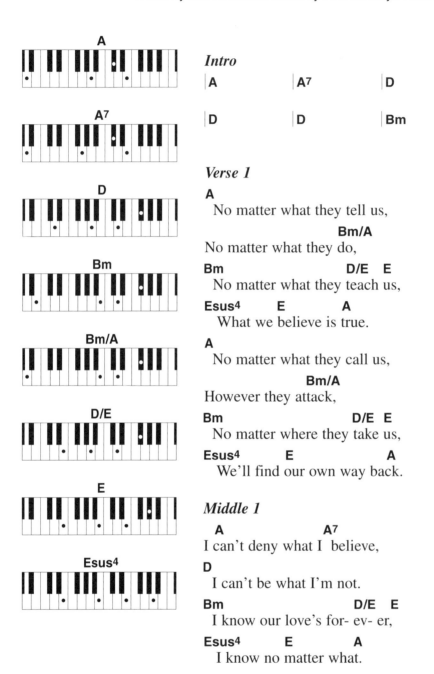

Intro

| A | A7 | D | D |
| D | D | Bm | A |

Verse 1

A
  No matter what they tell us,
                           Bm/A
No matter what they do,
Bm   D/E   E
  No matter what they teach us,
Esus4   E   A
  What we believe is true.

A
  No matter what they call us,
                   Bm/A
However they attack,
Bm   D/E   E
  No matter where they take us,
Esus4   E   A
  We'll find our own way back.

Middle 1

  A   A7
I can't deny what I believe,
D
  I can't be what I'm not.
Bm   D/E   E
  I know our love's for- ev- er,
Esus4   E   A
  I know no matter what.

Verse 2

A
  If only tears were laughter,
           Bm/A
If only night was day,
Bm   **D/E** **E**
  If only prayers were ans - wered,
Esus⁴   **E**   **A**
  Then we would hear God say.

A
  No matter what they tell you,
           Bm/A
No matter what they do,
Bm   **D/E** **E**
  No matter what they teach you,
Esus⁴   **E**   **A**
  What you believe is true.

Middle 2

    A   **A⁷**
And I will keep you safe and strong
D
  And sheltered from the storm.
Bm   **D/E** **E**
  No matter where it's barren
Esus⁴   **E**   **A**
  Our dream is being born.

Instrumental

|C |C |C |Dm | Dm |Dm/G G |G |C F/C ‖

Verse 3

C   **F/C**
  No matter who they follow,
C   **Dm**
  No matter where they lead,
           F/G **G**
No matter how they judge us,
Gsus⁴   **G**   **C**
  I'll be every one you need.

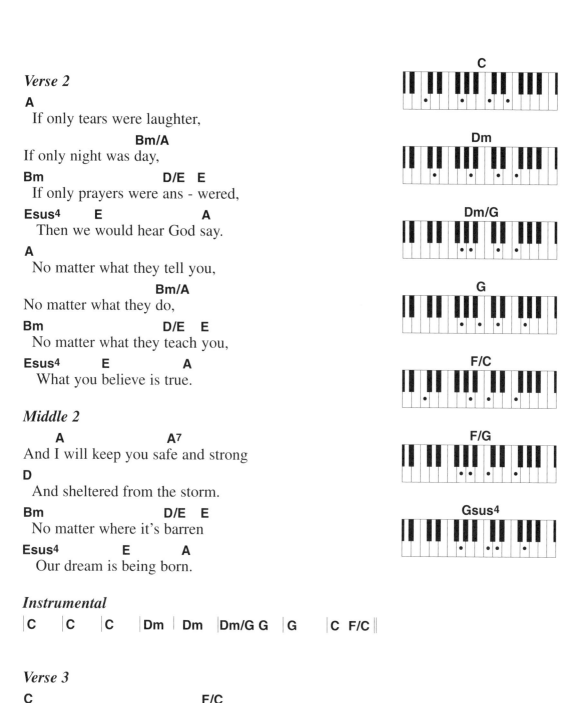

C

Dm

Dm/G

G

F/C

F/G

Gsus⁴

more chords overleaf...

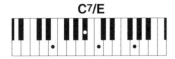

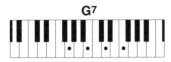

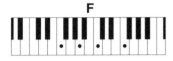

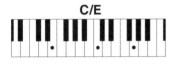

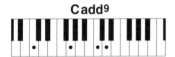

Bridge 3

      C   C7/E
No matter if the sun don't shine

F   C/E
  Or if the skies are blue.

Dm   F/G   G7
  No matter what the ending,

Gsus4   G7   C
   My life began with you.

Bridge 4

   C   C7/E
I can't deny what I   believe,

F   C/E
  I can't be what I'm not.

Dm   G7
  I know this love's forever,

                                     Cadd9
That's all that matters now, no matter what.

Outro

‖: Cadd9
  No, no matter, no.

                      :‖ *Repeat to fade*
No, no matter what.

Maria

Words & Music by Jimmy Destri

A5 (chord diagram)

Intro

| A5 | E | F#5 | E5 | |
| A5 | E5 | D5 | D5 | ||

E (chord diagram)

Verse 1

  A   E
She moves like she don't care;
F#m   D
Smooth as silk, cool as air.
A E   D
Ooh, it makes you wanna cry.
  A   E
She doesn't know your name
    F#m   D
And your heart beats like a subway train.
A E   D
Ooh, it makes you wanna die.

F#5 (chord diagram)

E5 (chord diagram)

Bridge 1

     E   F#m
Ooh, don't you wanna take her
D   E   F#m
 Or wanna make her all your own?

D5 (chord diagram)

Chorus 1

  A E/G#   F#m D
Maria, you've gotta see her,
  A   E   D
Go insane and out of your mind.
  A E/G# F#m D
Regina, ave Maria
  A   E   D
A million and one candle lights.

A (chord diagram)

F#m (chord diagram)

D (chord diagram)

E/G# (chord diagram)

more chords overleaf…

Verse 2

```
      A                       E
I've seen this thing before
   F♯m                    D
In my best friend and the boy next door.
A        E                  D
Fool for love and fool on fire.
      A                       E
You won't come in from the rain,
       F♯m                D
She's oceans runnin' down the drain,
A        E          D
Blue as ice and desire.
```

Bridge 2

```
            E                    F♯m
Don't you wanna make her?
D                E                F♯m
Ooh, don't you wanna take her home?
```

Chorus 2

```
      A  E/G♯                 F♯m      D
Maria,     you've gotta see her,
      A          E                 D
Go insane and out of your mind.
      A    E/G♯        F♯m     D
Regina,     ave Maria
      A          E                 D
A million and one candle lights.
```

Bridge 3

```
D                  E                    F♯m
Ooh, don't you wanna break her?
D                  E                  F♯m
Ooh, don't you wanna take her home?
```

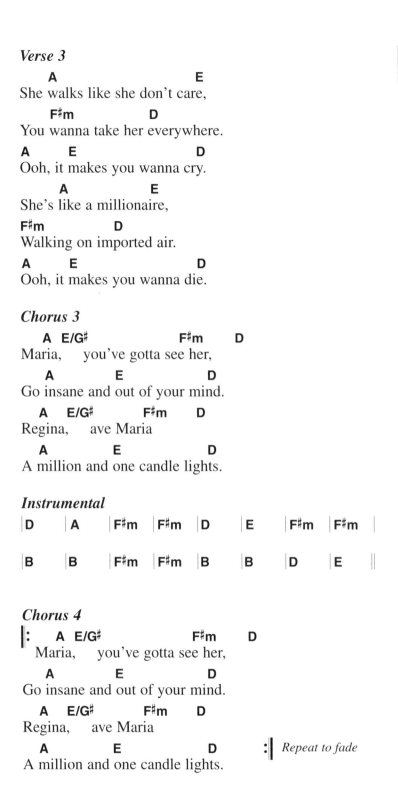

B

Verse 3

   A   E
She walks like she don't care,

   F♯m   D
You wanna take her everywhere.

A   E   D
Ooh, it makes you wanna cry.

      A   E
She's like a millionaire,

F♯m   D
Walking on imported air.

A   E   D
Ooh, it makes you wanna die.

Chorus 3

   A E/G♯   F♯m   D
Maria,   you've gotta see her,

    A   E   D
Go insane and out of your mind.

   A   E/G♯   F♯m   D
Regina,   ave Maria

   A   E   D
A million and one candle lights.

Instrumental

| D | A | F♯m | F♯m | D | E | F♯m | F♯m |

| B | B | F♯m | F♯m | B | B | D | E | ‖

Chorus 4

‖:   A E/G♯   F♯m   D
  Maria,   you've gotta see her,

    A   E   D
Go insane and out of your mind.

   A   E/G♯   F♯m   D
Regina,   ave Maria

    A   E   D   :‖ *Repeat to fade*
A million and one candle lights.

Praise You

Words & Music by Norman Cook & Camille Yarborough

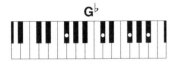

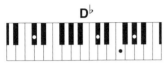

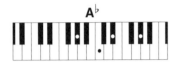

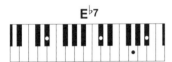

Intro

|G♭ D♭ A♭| |G♭ D♭ A♭| |

|G♭ D♭ A♭| |G♭ D♭ A♭| ‖

Verse 1

             G♭   D♭   A♭
We've come a long, long way together
          G♭   D♭   A♭
Through the hard times and the good.
       G♭ D♭   A♭
I have to celebrate you baby,
        G♭   D♭   A♭
I have to praise you like I should.

|G♭ D♭ A♭| |G♭ D♭ A♭| |

|G♭ D♭ A♭| |G♭ D♭ A♭| |

Instrumental

|G♭ D♭ A♭| |G♭ D♭ A♭| |

|G♭ D♭ A♭| |G♭ D♭ A♭| |

| N.C. | N.C. | N.C. | N.C.   ‖

Link 1

|G♭ D♭ A♭| |G♭ D♭ A♭| |

|G♭ D♭ A♭| |G♭ D♭ A♭| ‖

Verse 2

      G♭   **D♭**   **A♭**
We've come a long, long way together
      G♭   **D♭**   **A♭**
Through the hard times and the good.
    G♭ **D♭**   **A♭**
I have to celebrate you baby,
    G♭   **D♭** **A♭**
I have to praise you like I should.

Chorus 2

    G♭   **D♭** **A♭**
I have to praise you,
    G♭   **D♭** **A♭**
I have to praise you,
    G♭   **D♭** **A♭**
I have to praise you,
    G♭   **D♭**   **A♭**
I have to praise you like I should.
     E♭7   **A♭ D♭** |**E♭7 A♭ D♭** |**E♭7 A♭ D♭** |**E♭7**
I have to praise you,
A♭   **D♭ E♭7**   **A♭ D♭** |**E♭7 A♭ D♭** |**E♭7 A♭ D♭** |**E♭7**
I have to praise you.
A♭   **D♭ (E♭7)**
I have to praise you
 E♭7   **A♭**   **D♭**
(Na na na__ na na na
E♭7   **A♭**   **D♭**
Na na na__ na na na
E♭7   **A♭**   **D♭**
Na na na__ na na na
E♭7   **A♭**   **D♭**
Na na na__ na na na
E♭7   **A♭**   **D♭**
Na na na__ na na na
E♭7   **A♭**   **D♭**
Na na na__ na na na
E♭7   **A♭**   **D♭**
Na na na__ na na na
E♭7   **(A♭** **D♭)**
Na na na na.)

33

Link 2

D♭   A♭ G♭   D♭ A♭| G♭| D♭ A♭| G♭|

I have to praise you.

G♭   D♭ A♭| G♭| D♭ A♭| |

|N.C. |N.C. |N.C. |N.C.   ‖

Verse 3

                      G♭   D♭   A♭

We've come a long, long way together

                   G♭   D♭   A♭

Through the hard times and the good.

               G♭   D♭   A♭

I have to celebrate you baby,

                N.C.

I have to praise you like I should.

|N.C. |N.C. |N.C. |N.C.   ‖

Chorus 3

                G♭   D♭ A♭

I have to praise you,

                G♭   D♭ A♭

I have to praise you,

                G♭   D♭ A♭

I have to praise you,

                G♭   D♭ A♭

I have to praise you,

                G♭   D♭ A♭

I have to praise you,

                G♭   D♭ A♭

I have to praise you,

                G♭   D♭ A♭

I have to praise you,

               G♭   D♭   A♭

I have to praise you like I should.

        E♭7   A♭ D♭ |E♭7 A♭ D♭ |E♭7 A♭ D♭ |E♭7

I have to praise you,

A♭   D♭ E♭7   A♭ D♭ |E♭7 A♭ D♭ |E♭7 A♭ D♭ |E♭7

I have to praise you.

Outro

‖: A♭   D♭ (E♭7)

   I have to praise you.

 E♭7   A♭   D♭

(Na na na__ na na na,

E♭7   A♭   D♭

Na na na__ na na na,

E♭7   A♭   D♭

Na na na__ na na na,

E♭7   (A♭ D♭)   :‖ *Play 4 times*

Na na na na.)

A♭   D♭ N.C. |N.C.

I have to praise you.

‖: N.C. |N.C.   :‖ *Repeat to fade*

Teardrop

Words & Music by Robert del Naja, Grantley Marshall, Andrew Vowles & Elisabeth Fraser

Asus⁴

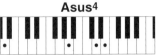

G⁶sus²

Dsus²

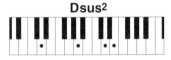

Fmaj⁷(add¹³)

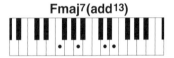

G

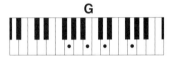

G⁶add⁹

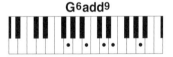

Asus⁴₂

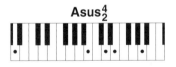

F

Intro

| N.C. | N.C. | N.C. | N.C. |

| Asus⁴ | Asus⁴ | Asus⁴ | Asus⁴ | Asus⁴ | Asus⁴ | Asus⁴ | Asus⁴ |

| Asus⁴ | G⁶sus² | Dsus² | Asus⁴ | G⁶sus² | Dsus² ‖

Verse 1

Asus⁴   G⁶sus²
Love, love is a verb, love is a doing word,

Dsus²   Asus⁴
Fearless on my breath.

Asus⁴   G⁶sus²
Gentle impulsion shakes me, makes me lighter,

Dsus²   Asus⁴
Fearless on my breath.

Fmaj⁷(add¹³)
Teardrop on the fire,

G⁶sus²   Asus⁴
Fearless on my breath.

Bridge

| N.C. | N.C. | N.C. | N.C. |

Verse 2

Asus⁴   G⁶sus²
The light of the day, black flowers blossom,

Dsus²   Asus⁴
Fearless on my breath.

Fmaj⁷(add¹³)
Black flowers blossom,

G⁶sus²   Asus⁴   Fmaj⁷(add¹³)
Fearless on my breath.

Dsus2
Teardrop on the fire,

G6sus2   **Asus4**
Fearless on my…

Link

‖: N.C. | N.C. | N.C. | N.C.   :‖

Verse 3

Asus4   **G6sus2**
Water is my eye, most faithful mirror,

Dsus2   **Asus4**
Fearless on my breath.

Asus4   **G6sus2**
Teardrop on the fire of a confession,

Dsus2   **Asus4**
Fearless on my breath.

Fmaj7(add13)
Most faithful mirror,

G6sus2   **Asus4**
Fearless on my breath.

Fmaj7(add13)
Teardrop on the fire.

G   **Fmaj7(add13)** | **Asus4** | **Fmaj7(add13)** |
Fearless on my breath.

| **G6sus2** | **Asus4** | **Fmaj7(add13)** | **G6sus2** | **Asus4** |

        Fmaj7(add13)   **G6add9**
You're stumbling in the dark,_____

            Asus$_2^4$
You're stumbling in the dark._____

Outro

‖: N.C. | N.C. | N.C. | N.C.   :‖

‖: **Fmaj7(add13)** | **G6sus2** | **G6sus2** | **G6sus2** :‖

| **Fmaj7(add13)** | **G6sus2** | **G6sus2** | **G6sus2** | **F** |

37

Runaway

Words & Music by Andrea Corr, Caroline Corr, Sharon Corr & Jim Corr

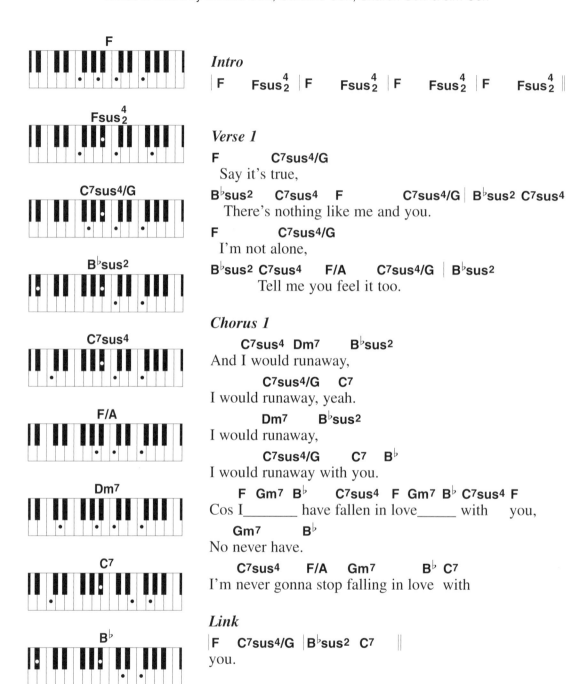

F

Fsus$_2^4$

C⁷sus⁴/G

B♭sus2

C⁷sus⁴

F/A

Dm7

C7

B♭

Intro

| F   Fsus$_2^4$ | F   Fsus$_2^4$ | F   Fsus$_2^4$ | F   Fsus$_2^4$ ||

Verse 1

F   C⁷sus⁴/G
 Say it's true,

B♭sus2 C⁷sus⁴ F   C⁷sus⁴/G | B♭sus2 C⁷sus⁴
 There's nothing like me and you.

F   C⁷sus⁴/G
 I'm not alone,

B♭sus2 C⁷sus⁴   F/A   C⁷sus⁴/G | B♭sus2
    Tell me you feel it too.

Chorus 1

     C⁷sus⁴ Dm7   B♭sus2
And I would runaway,

     C⁷sus⁴/G   C7
I would runaway, yeah.

       Dm7   B♭sus2
I would runaway,

     C⁷sus⁴/G   C7 B♭
I would runaway with you.

     F Gm7 B♭   C⁷sus⁴ F Gm7 B♭ C⁷sus⁴ F
Cos I_____ have fallen in love_____ with   you,

     Gm7   B♭
No never have.

     C⁷sus⁴ F/A Gm7   B♭ C7
I'm never gonna stop falling in love with

Link

| F C⁷sus⁴/G | B♭sus2 C7 ||
you.

Verse 2

F   C7sus4/G
  Close the door,

B♭sus2 C7sus4   F   C7sus4/G | B♭sus2 C7sus4
   Lay down upon the floor

F   C7sus4/G
  And by candlelight

B♭sus2   C7sus4   F/A   C7sus4/G | B♭sus2
   Make love to me through the night.

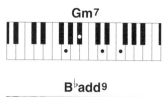

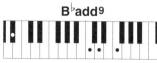

Chorus 2

     C7sus4 Dm7   B♭sus2
Cos I have runaway,

       C7sus4/G   C7
I have runaway, yeah, yeah.

     Dm7   B♭sus2
I have runaway, runaway

     C7sus4/G   C7 B♭
I have runaway with you.

   F Gm7 B♭   C7sus4 F Gm7 B♭ C7sus4 F
Cos I_____ have fallen in love_____ with you,

   Gm7   B♭
No never have.

   C7sus4   F/A   Gm7   B♭ C7 F   C7sus4/G
I'm never gonna stop falling in love with you,_____

   B♭add9   C7sus4
With you my love,

C7
With

Link 2

|F |C7sus4/G |B♭add9 |C7sus4
  you.

more chords overleaf...

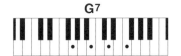

G7

Chorus 3

     C7   **Dm7**   **B♭sus2**
And I would runaway,

       C7sus4/G   **C7**
I would runaway, yeah.

      Dm7   **B♭sus2**
I would runaway,

      C7sus4/G   **C7** **B♭**
I would runaway with you.

    F Gm7 B♭   **C7sus4 F Gm7 B♭ C7sus4 F**
Cos I_____ have fallen in love_____ with   you,

   Gm7   **B♭**
No never have.

    C7sus4   **F/A**   **Gm7**   **B♭ C7**
I'm never gonna stop falling in love,

    F Gm7 B♭   **C7sus4 F Gm7 B♭ C7sus4 F**
Cos I_____ have fallen in love_____ with   you.

   Gm7   **B♭**
No, never have,

    C7sus4   **F/A**   **Gm7**   **B♭ C7**
I'm never gonna stop fallin' in love with

Outro

‖: **F**   **G7** | **B♭**
  you,

C7   **Dm7 G7**   **B♭ C7**   :‖   *Repeat to fade*
With you, my love,   with

2 Become 1

Words & Music by Victoria Adams, Melanie Brown, Emma Bunton,
Melanie Chisholm, Geri Halliwell, Matt Rowe & Richard Stannard

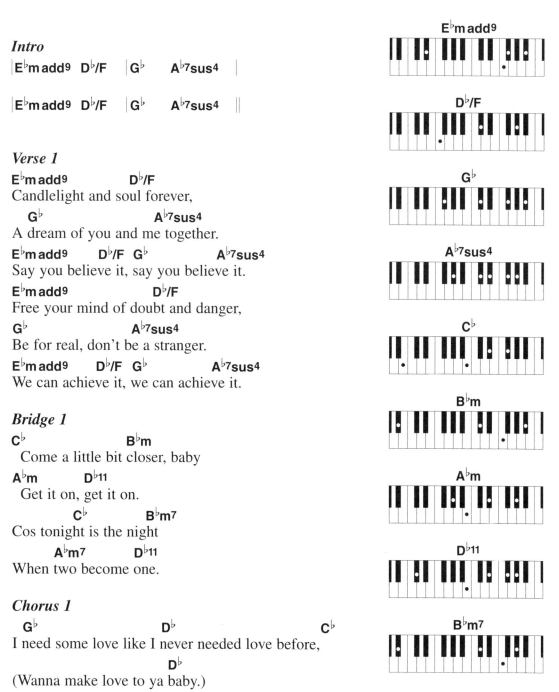

Intro

| E♭madd9 D♭/F |G♭   A♭7sus4 |

| E♭madd9 D♭/F |G♭   A♭7sus4 ||

Verse 1

E♭madd9   D♭/F
Candlelight and soul forever,
  G♭   A♭7sus4
A dream of you and me together.
E♭madd9   D♭/F G♭   A♭7sus4
Say you believe it, say you believe it.
E♭madd9   D♭/F
Free your mind of doubt and danger,
G♭   A♭7sus4
Be for real, don't be a stranger.
E♭madd9   D♭/F G♭   A♭7sus4
We can achieve it, we can achieve it.

Bridge 1

C♭   B♭m
  Come a little bit closer, baby
A♭m   D♭11
  Get it on, get it on.
       C♭   B♭m7
Cos tonight is the night
     A♭m7   D♭11
When two become one.

Chorus 1

  G♭   D♭   C♭
I need some love like I never needed love before,
               D♭
(Wanna make love to ya baby.)

more chords overleaf…

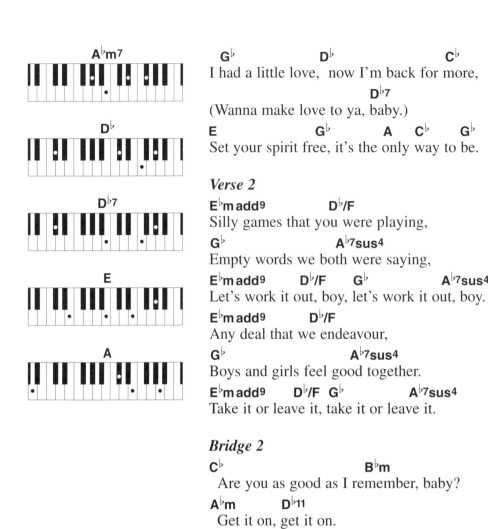

A♭m7

D♭

D♭7

E

A

G♭   D♭   C♭
I had a little love, now I'm back for more,
                            D♭7
(Wanna make love to ya, baby.)
E   G♭   A C♭   G♭
Set your spirit free, it's the only way to be.

Verse 2
E♭m add9   D♭/F
Silly games that you were playing,
G♭   A♭7sus4
Empty words we both were saying,
E♭m add9   D♭/F   G♭   A♭7sus4
Let's work it out, boy, let's work it out, boy.
E♭m add9   D♭/F
Any deal that we endeavour,
G♭   A♭7sus4
Boys and girls feel good together.
E♭m add9   D♭/F G♭   A♭7sus4
Take it or leave it, take it or leave it.

Bridge 2
C♭   B♭m
  Are you as good as I remember, baby?
A♭m   D♭11
  Get it on, get it on.
         C♭   B♭m7
Cos tonight is the night
      A♭m7   D♭11
When two become one.

Chorus 2

G♭   D♭   C♭
I need some love like I never needed love before,
                          D♭
(Wanna make love to ya baby.)
G♭   D♭   C♭
I had a little love, now I'm back for more,
                          D♭7
(Wanna make love to ya, baby.)
E   G♭   A C♭   G♭
Set your spirit free, it's the only way to be.

Link

|E♭m   D♭ |C♭ |E♭m   D♭ |C♭

                          Oh,___ oh.___

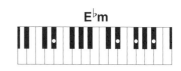

E♭m

D♭maj7

Bridge 3

C♭   B♭m
  Be a little bit wiser, baby

A♭m   D♭11
  Put it on, put it on.

                C♭   B♭m7
Cos tonight is the night

        A♭m7   D♭11
When two become one.

Chorus 3

  G♭   D♭   C♭
I need some love like I never needed love before,

                      D♭
(Wanna make love to ya baby.)

  G♭   D♭   C♭
I had a little love, now I'm back for more,

                    D♭maj7
(Wanna make love to ya, baby.)

  G♭   D♭   C♭
I need some love like I never needed love before,

                    D♭
(Wanna make love to ya baby.)

  G♭   D♭   C♭
I had a little love, now I'm back for more,

                    D♭7
(Wanna make love to ya, baby.)

E   G♭
Set your spirit free,

‖:   A   C♭   G♭   :‖   *Repeat to fade*
  It's the only way to be

When You're Gone

Words & Music by Bryan Adams & Eliot Kennedy

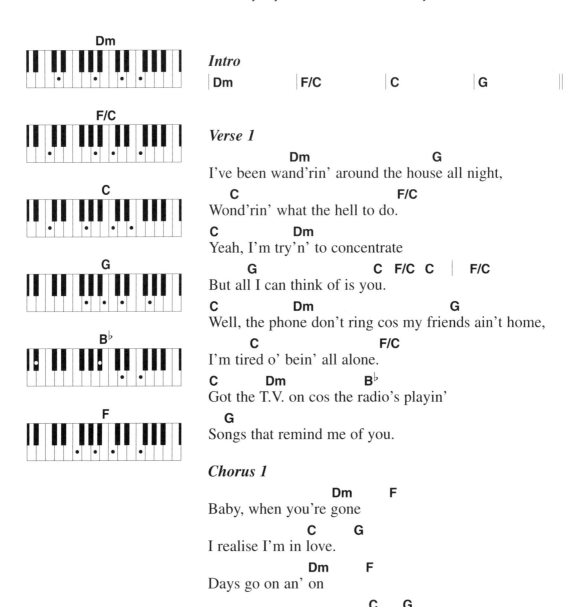

Dm

F/C

C

G

B♭

F

Intro

| Dm |F/C |C |G   ‖

Verse 1

            Dm   G
I've been wand'rin' around the house all night,
      C   F/C
Wond'rin' what the hell to do.
C   Dm
Yeah, I'm try'n' to concentrate
         G   C   F/C   C | F/C
But all I can think of is you.
C   Dm   G
Well, the phone don't ring cos my friends ain't home,
       C   F/C
I'm tired o' bein' all alone.
C   Dm   B♭
Got the T.V. on cos the radio's playin'
    G
Songs that remind me of you.

Chorus 1

           Dm   F
Baby, when you're gone
        C   G
I realise I'm in love.
         Dm   F
Days go on an' on
               C   G
And the nights just seem so__ long.
             Dm   F
Even food don't taste that good,
          C   G
Drink ain't doin' what it should.

<pre>
        Dm   B♭
Things just feel so wrong,
                G
Baby, when you're gone.
</pre>

Verse 2

<pre>
            Dm   G
I've been drivin' up and down these streets
  C   F/C
Tryin' to find somewhere to go.
C   Dm
Yeah, I'm lookin' for a familiar face
             G   C F/C C | F/C
But there's no one I know.
C   Dm   G
Oh, this is torture, this is pain,
      C   F/C
It feels like I'm gonna go insane.
C   Dm   B♭
I hope you're comin' back real soon
      G
Cos I don't know what to do.
</pre>

Chorus 2

As Chorus 1

Bridge

<pre>
|Dm |G |C |C |Dm |G |C |C |

|Dm |G |C |C |Dm |B♭ |G |G ||
</pre>

Chorus 3

As Chorus 1

Outro

<pre>
                   Dm
Oh baby, when you're gone,
B♭   F
  Yes baby, when you're gone.
</pre>

Why Does It Always Rain On Me?

Words & Music by Fran Healy

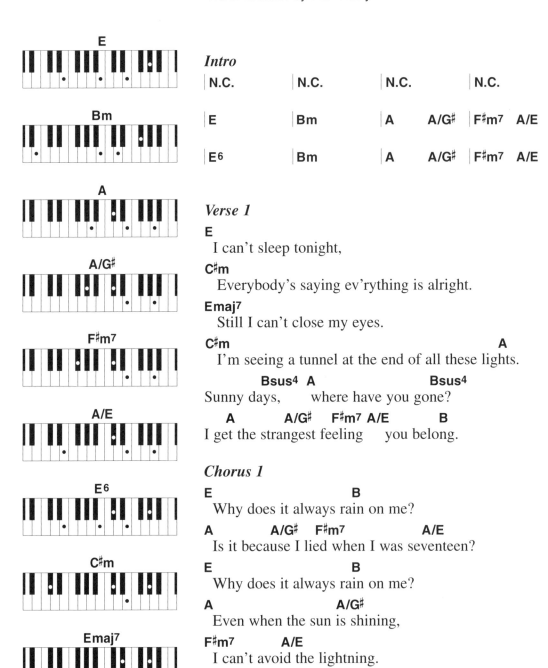

Intro

| N.C. | N.C. | N.C. | N.C. | |

| E | Bm | A   A/G# | F#m7   A/E | |

| E6 | Bm | A   A/G# | F#m7   A/E | ‖

Verse 1

E
   I can't sleep tonight,
C#m
   Everybody's saying ev'rything is alright.
Emaj7
   Still I can't close my eyes.
C#m   A
   I'm seeing a tunnel at the end of all these lights.
                 Bsus4 A   Bsus4
Sunny days,   where have you gone?
     A   A/G#   F#m7 A/E   B
I get the strangest feeling   you belong.

Chorus 1

E   B
   Why does it always rain on me?
A   A/G#   F#m7   A/E
   Is it because I lied when I was seventeen?
E   B
   Why does it always rain on me?
A   A/G#
   Even when the sun is shining,
F#m7   A/E
   I can't avoid the lightning.

Verse 2

E
  I can't stand myself,

C#m
  I'm being held up by invisible men.

Emaj7
  Still life on a shelf when

C#m   **A**
  I got my mind on something else.

         Bsus4 A   **Bsus4**
Sunny days,   where have you gone?

    A   **A/G#**   **F#m7 A/E**   **B**
I get the strangest feeling   you belong.

Chorus 2

As Chorus 1

Middle

   C#m   **E/B**
Oh, where did the blue sky go?

   C#m   **E/B**   **D   D/C#** | **Bm7**
Oh, why is it raining so?__

     D/A   Bsus4 | **B**
It's so cold.

Verse 3

As Verse 1

Chorus 3

E   **B**
  Why does it always rain on me?

A   **A/G#**   **F#m7**   **A/E**
  Is it because I lied when I was seventeen?

E   **B**
  Why does it always rain on me?

A   **A/G#**
  Even when the sun is shining,

F#m7   **A/E**
  I can't avoid the lightning.

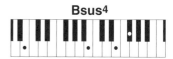
Bsus4

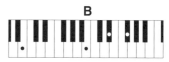
B

E/B

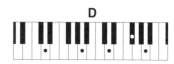
D

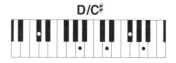
D/C#

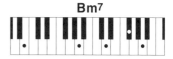
Bm7

D/A

Middle 2

  C#m   E/B
Oh, where did the blue sky go?

  C#m   E/B   D D/C# | Bm7
Oh, why is it raining so?__

    D/A Bsus4 | B
It's so cold.

Chorus 4

E   B
  Why does it always rain on me?

A   A/G#   F#m7   A/E
  Is it because I lied when I was seventeen?

E   B
  Why does it always rain on me?

A   A/G#
  Even when the sun is shining,

F#m7   A/E   E
  I can't avoid the lightning.

Outro

                Bm   A A/G# | F#m7 A/E
Why does it always rain on me?

E6   Bm A A/G# | F#m7 A/E | E
  Why does it always rain on_____ oh.____